Long Ago and Today

by Quinn Douglas

SCHOOL PUBLISHERS

Cover ©Photolibrary.com; 3 ©Getty Images/Time & Life Pictures; 4 ©Getty Images; 5 ©PhotoDisc; 6 ©Getty Images; 7 ©Photolibrary.com; 8 ©Australian Picture Library; 9 ©Photolibrary.com; 10 ©Getty Images; 11 ©Lindsay Edwards Photography; 12 ©Getty Images/Time & Life Pictures; 13–14 ©Photolibrary.com.

Copyright © by Harcourt, Inc.

All rights reserved. No part of this publication may be reproduced or transmitted in any form or by any means, electronic or mechanical, including photocopy, recording, or any information storage and retrieval system, without permission in writing from the publisher.

Requests for permission to make copies of any part of the work should be addressed to School Permissions and Copyrights, Harcourt, Inc., 6277 Sea Harbor Drive, Orlando, Florida 32887-6777. Fax: 407-345-2418.

HARCOURT and the Harcourt Logo are trademarks of Harcourt, Inc., registered in the United States of America and/or other jurisdictions.

Printed in Mexico

ISBN 10: 0-15-350417-X
ISBN 13: 978-0-15-350417-4

Ordering Options
ISBN 10: 0-15-350332-7 (Grade 2 Below-Level Collection)
ISBN 13: 978-0-15-350332-0 (Grade 2 Below-Level Collection)
ISBN 10: 0-15-357437-2 (package of 5)
ISBN 13: 978-0-15-357437-5 (package of 5)

If you have received these materials as examination copies free of charge, Harcourt School Publishers retains title to the materials and they may not be resold. Resale of examination copies is strictly prohibited and is illegal.

Possession of this publication in print format does not entitle users to convert this publication, or any portion of it, into electronic format.

3 4 5 6 7 8 9 10   050   15 14 13 12 11 10 09 08

Imagine that you lived a long
time ago. What would you and your
friends have done for fun?

Long ago, children played board games.

Today, many children still play
board games.

Long ago, children listened to their favorite songs on the radio.

Today, children also listen
to music. Many children play
their favorite songs on small
music players.

Long ago, books cost a lot of money. Many families could buy only a few books. Children read the same books over and over again.

Today, books are easy to get.
Children may buy books or borrow
them from school or city libraries.

Long ago, girls often helped
their mothers cook.

Today, both boys and girls help
their mothers and fathers cook.

Long ago, children played
sports. They played in the
neighborhood with other children.

Today, many children still play sports. Some sports are played at different times of the year.

Children today still do many
of the fun things that children did
long ago. What fun things do you
and your friends like to do?

Think Critically

1. What are some things that children today like to do that children long ago also liked to do?

2. Why did children long ago read the same books again and again?

3. Where did children long ago often play sports?

4. Why do you think the author wrote this book?

5. What activity from the book would you like to do? Why?

 **Social Studies**

Make a Chart Make a chart with the heads: *Today* and *Long Ago*. Write three sentences under each head about life today and long ago.

School-Home Connection Talk to a family member about what children long ago used to do to have fun and what children do today to have fun.

Word Count: 174